Four Freckled Frogs

a book about consonants

Ruth Thomson

Thameside Press

Distributed in the United States by
Smart Apple Media
1980 Lookout Drive
North Mankato, MN 56003

ISBN 1-930643-60-8

Library of Congress Control Number: 2001088833

Series editors: Mary-Jane Wilkins, Stephanie Turnbull
Designers: Rachel Hamdi, Angie Allison, Holly Mann
Illustrators: Louise Comfort, Charlotte Hard, Holly Mann
Educational consultants: Pie Corbett, Poet and Consultant
   to the English National Literacy Strategy; Sarah Mullen,
   Literacy Consultant

Printed in Hong Kong

9 8 7 6 5 4 3 2 1

Four Freckled Frogs

a book about consonants

This beautiful book will help lay the early foundations for reading. Young children love words and often invent their own, savoring the sounds. They will enjoy having the rhymes and sentences read to them, and spotting objects in the pictures that start with the same sound.

Each page introduces a certain sound, so that children become aware of the different sounds that letters make. Early play with sounds, rhymes, and letters is fun and a fundamental beginning to becoming a reader.

Children are never too young to enjoy words, letters, and sounds. They make the pathway to reading both simple and joyful.

Pie Corbett

Pie Corbett

Poet and Consultant to the
English National Literacy Strategy

There are games to reinforce children's learning on page 30. You will then find a list of words illustrated in the book on pages 31 and 32.

st

Steve stops and stares at the ghost on the stage.

st

ghost

stick

steps

chest

star

stage

statue

nest

stool

What is the ghost carrying?
What is the boy picking up?

tr

The truck is stuck on the train tracks.

tr

tractor

truck

triangle

trumpet

tree

tray

trombone

trunk

tricycle

What musical instruments can you see?
What is the girl carrying?

train

pr

The princess is not impressed by presents.

princess

fingerprints

apricot

prince

prize

present

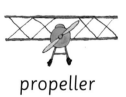

propeller

primrose

Who is trying to impress the princess?

What can you see on the top shelf?

6

gr

grandpa

Grandpa grabs greedy grasshoppers.

gr

grasshopper

greenhouse

green

grapes

grapefruit

grass

gray

grandma

gravel

What is in Grandpa's greenhouse?

What is Grandma holding?

fr

frog

frying pan

frost

fruit

Four freckled frogs are frying fresh fruit.

fr

fridge

freckles

frown

frame

What is on the wall?

What is the weather like?

 **cr**

The crafty crocodile crept after the crab.

cr

crocodile

crab

cry

crown

crowd

crane

crumbs

crutches

crayon

crate

Who is watching?

What is the baby doing?

The bridesmaid fell off
the broken brick bridge.

br

bridesmaid

bridge

bread

bracelet

branch

brown

brooch

broom

brick

What is the bridesmaid holding?
What jewelry is the bride wearing?

dr

The dreadful dragon drove the drummers out of town.

dr

dragon

drum

drummer

dress

drops

drake

dragonfly

drawbridge

What animals can you see?

What is the girl wearing?

11

Sl

The sleepy sloths slid slowly down the slope.

Sl

sled

slide

slope

slice

sleeve

slipper

sloth

sling

What are the sloths wearing?

What is the man eating?

pl

The plump plumber played with the platypus.

pl

platypus

plate

plank

pliers

plum

plump

plane

planet

plant

What is the plumber holding?

What are the children doing?

13

gl

The glamorous glutton owns a glossy glider.

gl

glider

glass

gloves

globe

glasses

glow-worm

What is the pilot holding?
What can you see on the chairs?

The fine fleet of boats floated through the flood.

fl fl

flag

flock

flower

fleet

flute

flame

flippers

butterfly

What are the children doing?
What instrument can you see?

bl

The blindfolded bear blunders into the blackberries.

blindfold

bluebell

blanket

blackberry

blue

blossom

black

blood

What is the blushing bear doing?
Who is perched in the tree?

clown

cloud

clarinet

club

Clever clowns go
to clown classes.

clock

cliff

cloth

What are the clowns doing?
What can you see out of the window?

sk

skeleton

sk

skunk

mask

skirt

skyscrapers

basket

skull

skis

What are the skeletons wearing?
What can you see in the distance?

sp

The spotted spider ate a spoonful of spaghetti.

sp

spider

spaghetti

spoon

spaceship

sparrow

spout

sponge

spear

What else can you see in the spooky room?
What is outside?

SW

The swallows swooped over the swimmers.

SW

swimmer

swallow

swimsuit

swan

swimming pool

swing

sweatshirt

What other bird can you see?

What are all the children doing?

str

str

The ostrich strolled
down the street.

ostrich

streamers

strongman

strawberry

string

stripes

stretcher

What are people eating?

What is the cat playing with?

The **scruffy** **scarecrow** rode to **school**.

sc — scr

scarecrow

scarlet

school

scarf

scooter

screw

screwdriver

What is the scarecrow riding?

What is he taking with him?

mp

The chimp played his trumpet at camp.

mp

chimpanzee

trampoline

lamp

stump

pump

hamper

swamp

trumpet

What are the chimps jumping on?

What is the chimp in the blue hat doing?

The ants climbed over the silent giant.

giant

fountain

mountain

paint

tent

plant

paintbrush

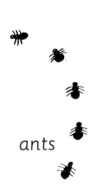

ants

What can you see in the distance?

Why is the man on a ladder?

 monkey

The monkey sprinkles ink on the bunk.

nk

 blanket

 bunk beds

 hankie

ink

 piggy bank

pink

 fish tank

What color is the ink?

What is on top of the trunk?

25

nd

panda

The kind panda hands out the cotton candy.

nd

bandstand

garland

hand

pond

cotton candy

island

sand

What can you see behind the girl?
What sort of day is it?

The bull with a bell bellowed at silly Billy.

bull

ball

hill

shell

bell

balloon

doll

wall

What color is Billy's t-shirt?

What can you see in the bull's field?

ing

Children bring the king all kinds of things.

ing

king

finger

ring

wing

swing

sling

earring

painting

What are the children bringing?
What is the queen doing?

28

ff ff

The puffin ate a muffin with toffee and some coffee.

puffin

coffee

cliff

muffin

giraffe

toffee

What is on the table?

What is going on outside?

Notes for parents and teachers

Once children are aware of consonant blends, they can start looking for them anywhere. Ask them to pick them out in story books, nursery rhymes, and songs. For example, can they hear whether there are any consonant blends in "Three Blind Mice"?

Here are three activities to help children hear consonant blends.

Sorting game

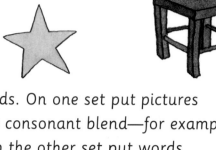

Make two sets of picture cards. On one set put pictures of items that begin with one consonant blend—for example, a star, a stool, and steps. On the other set put words beginning with a different blend—for example, a sleeve, a slide, and a sled. Ask the child to say each word, listen to the sound, and then sort the cards into two separate piles.

Find the blend

Put a group of objects on a tray, some of which start with the same consonant blend. Hold up each object. The child says its name (if their pronounciation is unclear they can repeat the word after you). If the word starts or ends with the consonant blend they place it in a pile. If it doesn't, it stays on the tray.

Sentences

Make up sentences based on a consonant blend and chant them, e.g. the trembling train trapped the tractor. Have fun! The game works best if the sentences are nonsense.

Word list

Here are all the words illustrated in this book.

bl
(p. 16)
black
blackberry
blackbird
blade
blanket
bleat
bleed
blind man's
  buff
blindfold
blood
blossom
blow
blue
bluebell
blunder
blush

br
(p. 10)
bracelet
branch
bread
breakfast
breeze
briar
brick
bride
bridegroom
bridesmaid
bridge
bright
broken
brooch
brook
broom
brown
brush

cl
(p. 17)
clap
clarinet
class
classroom
clean
clever
cliff
climb
cloak
clock
closet
cloth
clothes
cloud
clown
clowning
club
clumsy

cr
(p. 9)
crab
crafty
crane
crash
  helmet
crate
crawl
crayon
creep
crocodile
crowd
crown
crumbs
crutches
cry

dr
(p. 11)
dragon
dragonfly
drainpipe
drake
drawbridge
dreadful
dress
drink
drizzle
droop
drop
drum
drummer
dry

ff
(p. 29)
cliff
coffee
coffeepot
cuff
giraffe
huff
muffin
puff
puffin
toffee

fl
(p. 15)
butterfly
flag
flame
flap
flautist
fleet
flipper

float
flock
flood
floppy
florist
flower
fluffy
flute
flutter
fly

fr
(p. 8)
frame
freckle
freezer
fresh
fridge
friendly
frill
frog
frost
frown
frozen
fruit
fry
frying pan

gl
(p. 14)
glad
glamorous
glass
glasses
gleam
glider
glisten
glitter

globe
gloomy
glossy
glove
glow
glow-worm
glutton

gr
(p. 7)
grab
grandma
grandpa
grape
grapefruit
grass
grasshopper
gravel
gray
greedy
green
greenhouse
grin
grubby
grumpy

ing
(p. 28)
bring
drawing
earring
finger
icing
king
nothing
painting
ring
sing

sling
spring
swimming
  pool
swing
thing
wing

ll
(p. 27)
ball
balloon
bell
bellow
Billy
bull
call
doll
full
hill
holly
roll
shell
silly
tall
wall
well
yell
yellow

mp
(p. 23)

camp
chimpanzee
clump
grumpy
hamper
hump
jump
lamp
lump
plump
pump
stamp
stump
swamp
trample
trampoline
trumpet

nd
(p. 26)

band
bandstand
cotton
  candy
garland
hand
handle
island
kind
music stand
panda
pond
sand
stand
windy

nk
(p. 25)

ankle
blanket
bunk beds
donkey
drink

fish tank
hankie
ink
monkey
piggy bank
pink
plank
sprinkle
trunk
wink

nt
(p. 24)

ant
fountain
giant
mountain
paint
paintbrush
painter
parent
plant
point
silent
tent

pl
(p. 13)

plain
plane
planet
plank
plant
plaque
plate
platypus
play
playground
pleated
pliers
plum
plumber
plump

pr
(p. 6)

apricot
fingerprint
impress
present
pretty
prick
prickle
prickly
primrose
prince
princess
prize
propeller
proud

sc/scr
(p. 22)

scarecrow
scared
scarf
scarlet
school
schoolteacher
scooter
scowl
scream
screech
screw
screwdriver
scribble
scruffy

sk
(p. 18)

basket
mask
roller skate
skate
skeleton
ski
skinny
skirt
skull

skunk
sky
skyscraper

sl
(p. 12)

asleep
sled
sleepy
sleeve
slice
slide
sling
slip
slipper
slope
sloth
slowly
slug

sp
(p. 19)

space
spaceship
spaghetti
sparrow
spear
spell
spice
spider
spike
spill
spoke
sponge
spooky
spoon
spoonful
spot
spotted
spout

st
(p. 4)

chest
fist
ghost
lamppost
nest
stage
stand
star
stare
statue
step
Steve
stew
stick
stir
stone
stool
stop
stove

str
(p. 21)

ostrich
straight
strap
strawberry
streamer
street
stretcher
string
stripe
stroll
strong
strongman

sw
(p. 20)

swallow
swan
swap
sweat
sweatshirt
sweep
swim
swimmer
swimming
  pool
swimsuit
swing
swoop

tr
(p. 5)

track
tracksuit
tractor
train
tray
treasure
tree
triangle
tricycle
trio
triplet
trombone
trombonist
trophy
trousers
truck
trumpet
trumpeter
trunk